If Only You Knew Dahlin'

AF665102

The Aura of Rhymes

BookLeaf Publishing
India | USA | UK

If Only You Knew Dahlin' © 2021 The Aura Of Rhymes

All rights reserved.

No part of this publication may be reproduced, stored in a retrieval system, or transmitted, in any form or by any means, electronic, mechanical, photocopying, recording or otherwise, without the prior written permission of the presenters.

The Aura Of Rhymes asserts the moral right to be identified as author of this work.

Presentation by *BookLeaf Publishing*

Web: www.bookleafpub.com

E-mail: info@bookleafpub.com

ISBN: 9789358360080

First edition 2021

Preface

"To thine own self be true." — William Shakespeare

"As you start to walk on the way, the way appears." — Rumi

“Remember that wherever your heart is, there you will find your treasure” — Paulo Coelho

“Feel, he told himself, feel, feel, feel. Even if what you feel is pain, only let yourself feel.” — P. D. James

Dedicating my book to the universe and to everyone who is trying to make it in life, and most importantly, to my sister, who has been my greatest support, strength and mentor.

Unseen and Unheard!

A Blind girl's confession to her love!

Holding my hand, guiding me to a garden of roses,

He whispered, "Spiral your way into the synthetic of voices and noises,

Navigate through the patterns of braille textures."

I held his hand, to only feel the drips of his helplessness,

Smiling softly as I gasped into the spring air.

The softness of the fresh fragranced petals brushed against my fingers,

Feeling the senses running through my veins more than he could ever begin to imagine.

If only he could see the light in my darkness,

And hear the voices in my head,

He would not give me the stares of confusion.

True that, the mirror seems like nothing but just a word,

Waking up to a receded eyesight could be every reason to bleed,

I found my comfort through the silence of colours,

As my heart cried louder in the quiet stillness of the night,

The harmonies of the wind,

The warmth of the sun and change of tides.

Somehow the seasons seems to be more clearer in the shaded shadows,

I felt the pain in his tears trying to blend into the rain,

Indeed, he could feel the ones with vision,

For I am no stranger to the constant battles of dark revisions,

Though I felt his intricate precision,

I held his chest only to hear his sighs and highs,

I refused to surrender into the darkness of the blind,

Living in the creation of the world in my own mind!

Call It A Night!

Find your way into my naked chrysalis,

Let my generosity

Speak a tone of kindness,

A story I have once forgotten about,

A whisper the breeze once understood,

Midnight epiphany.

Just give me a reason to break this silence,

As the comfort in this closet sets to fade into a new glimpse of spring,

Feathers and leathers bent to the silky waves and teasing nights,

You were poison, destroyed by the weight of their tongues,

My love is not an unforgiven pain,

Resting in denial with where the pain lives.

How exposed am I to the fire in my throat
against the sacred spaces,

Let's just unleash onto our pomegranate cheeks
and call it a night, my dahlin'.

Questions of Unquestioned Questions!

Did you wake up to a morning where tears fall silently like floods which do not clear?

Encroaching dark clouds filling your life with fear,

Is agony from heartbreak too much for you to take?

Remorse from your regrets is a painful mistake,

How deep has sorrow poisoned your mind like a snake?

Would you embrace another day of your sombre life?

When your emotions collapsed with the state of suffering rife,

Aggravated and aggrieved, you sit staring at my name carved in stone,

Do you remember all the unconditional love that was shown?

Dahlin' how could you possibly spend a night on your own?

Tormented and tortured by your own loss,
hoping to feel my tender touch,

Is each minute that passes by far too much?

Is every moment of your silence driven by a rush?

Lost in the peak of your own pedestal,

Drifted to a flaming night of warmth so magical,

Questions after unquestioned questions,

I hear you whisper through the silent stars...

Painted Love

Time has painted the horizon,

Reliving those times of the cold sun, dark moon and blurred stars,

While I painted my heart from hues of moonstones.

He and I, his and hers, lingered through tokens of love,

He said love is love and yet whispered "who knows this ship is gonna wreck".

While the ship has sailed into the shady heart of the ocean,

You shall find me floating,

Suspended in the middle of the blue sapphire eyes water,

Exploring deeper within the hidden passages,

Carrying silenced messages of a beautiful love.

Lilac Haze

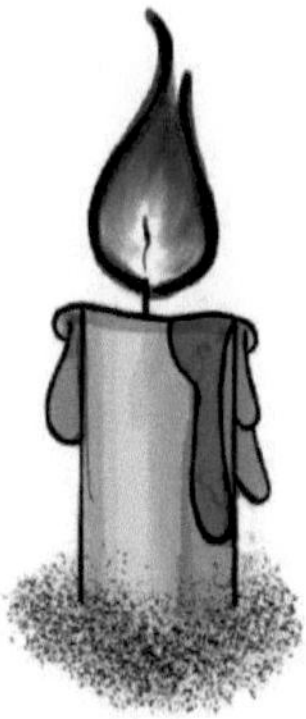

Sky full of candles,

Fresh wind breezing on my lips,

I drift to moon dreams

Eve of a diamond,

Glistening stars reflecting,

Golden rays to snooze

Soaring purple haze,

Of blissful cottons scattered,

Woven in the palms

Sweet lingers of sand,

Swept across the silver waves,

A rose with no thorns

Beaming under the shadows,

To bathe in lilac meadows

Poetic form: Haiku Sonnet
Which consists of 4 haiku as 5,7,5 syllables and one couplet of 7 syllables.

Foul Deception

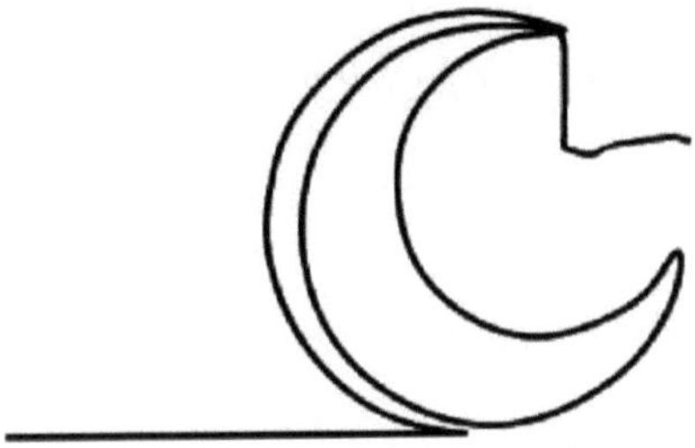

Under the never setting sky, left hooked,

I yearned for a morning yet so bright,

Floating in constitutional glory,

Uplift every beating time of beauty,

Mocking waves of sun in the horizon,

Playing cool, left astonished by the sight.

Chasing shadows as I dimmed my blurred sight,

Clearest moon tangled as it got me hooked,
Distanced candles that touched the horizon,
Clearing my fogged mind to a soul so bright,
Catching a second in glimpse of beauty,
Had no mercy for the touch of glory.

Mesmerized to a deceiving glory,
You were my shelter, beautified sight.
Am I supposed to count on that beauty,
Through constant tears and smiles which got me hooked?
Shameless tricks that burnt our dreams so bright,
As the ashes coloured the horizon.

Fading every hue from the horizon,
Shall I send my love in perfect glory?
Let you feel the sense in some form of bright,
A peaceful serenity in your sight?

You dare to feel the love I had you hooked,
You who refused to believe in beauty?

All you portrayed was just killer beauty,
Hard to find, simply lost in horizon,
Never to blame the blind ones who were hooked,
Wishing for eternal peace and glory,
Flipping to a different day's shocking sight,
Dancing to the pain as it remained bright.

Even in the darkness you glow so bright,
Cannons that wrote the tales of our beauty,
Cherishing the roses that wilt in sight,
Alarm beyond your touching horizon,
Whisper the sounds of our loving glory,
Declining the signs of us getting hooked.

Bright disguise hidden in the horizon,

Beauty banishing the lust of glory,

Hooked on a pleasant dry melodious sight.

Poetic Form: Sestina

(6 stanzas with 6 lines following an envoy. Pick 6 words and play around with it. Refrain of words as following; it should be 10 syllables per line.)

A- hooked

B- bright

C-glory

D-beauty

E-horizon

F-sight

First stanza : ABCDEF

Second stanza : FAEBDC

Third stanza : CFDABE

Fourth stanza : ECBFAD

Fifth stanza : DEACFB

Sixth stanza : BDFECA

Envoy : BE,DC,AF

Unfolded Dahlin'

Remember I have unfolded your scars,

When all kept on doubting your tinted hues,

Magnetized into your own rusty bars.

You simply sat among the dying stars,

As I engraved in your veins as a muse,

Remember I have unfolded your scars.

Lost beyond the lines of your own radars,

You sway in a sly beat as you confuse,

Magnetized into your own rusty bars.

Wasting your life as you lit them cigars,

Dressed in white to drift in the sand dunes,

Remember I have unfolded your scars.

You obsess with the thought of going far,

You left your stories under the cold bruise,

Magnetized into your own rusty bars.

Mid highs left as the only spark of ours,

And you have become an addictive fuse,

Remember I have unfolded your scars,

Magnetized into your own rusty bars.

Poetic Form : Villanelle

French poetic form with rhymes and refrains as following. Keeping in mind 5 tercet, 1 four line stanza, 19 lines with 10 syllables;

Rhyme scheme with refrains

b1, B, b2/ B , C, b1/ B, C, b1/ B, C, b2/ B, C, b1/ B, C, b1, b2.)

Dear Mother (Tribute to My Mother)

Mom,

I hope

I get to

See your shine, your

Fire, even after

We leave this unfair world

Behind. There is no telling

When you could strike the heart of the

Devil's trolls, walk away so swiftly,

Elegantly shielded us with patience.

Poetic Form: Etheree

It is a simple short poetic form consisting of 10 unrhymed lines with a syllable count of 1,2,3,4,5,6,7,8,9,10. To make it more creative, you could go from 10 to 1 or write a double Etheree as 1 to 10 and 10 to 1.

Wordless Romance

When

The nights

Were silent

And when I was

Lost in the jungle,

I found a piece of you

Hiding behind metaphors

Of broken love you have survived.

I heard your melodies of not to

Fall in the books of forgive and forget.

Still, it feels like an unfinished album,

A wordless romance of incomplete

Pages with black and white mornings

In the soft warmth of your arms.

I am found longing to

Meet your eyes, your lips,

Your touch, one last

Breath of time.

Till then,

Dream!

Poetic Form: Double Etheree

Fine Sarcasm

I've been watching you

Watching me, the salty smirk

Across the ocean,

Waving me with fine sarcasm.

Should I laugh or cry out loud?

Poetic Form: Tanka

Tanka is a Japanese verse, following the syllable count as 5/7/5/7/7.

Purple Blush

Touch of deep azure,

Neon dusts hover in silence,

Where roses do blush

Muse of purple haze,

Candles enlightening veins,

Rush into the wild

Poetic Form: Haiku (Double Haiku)
A Japanese form of poetry, no rhymes but follows a syllable count as 5,7,5. Haiku is written using the elements of nature.

Sky Stories

Question, can the moon be lonely?

Feasting on stars so unholy,

Move in galaxies,

Making memories,

Sky stories,

Unworldly.

Poetic Form: Clogyrnach
A welsh form consisting of 6 lines
syllable: 8,8,5,5,3,3 rhymes scheme as a,a,b,b,b,a.

Poetic Monster

You,

And your

Poetic

Lies, lost in the

Verses of poisoned roots of

Untouched souls,

Walking through the depths of white sapphire stars,

Manmade monsters,

Dancing to

Beats of

Love.

Poetic Form: Tetractys (Double Tetractys)

Tetractys should be atleast 5 lines with a syllable count 1,2,3,4,10. A double tetractys would be 1, 2, 3, 4, 10, 10, 4, 3, 2, 1. You could also go for a triple tetractys.

Despite The Path

Looking in the walkway frozen,

Muse in me on an empty night,

My sight undoubtedly hazen,

Opalescent path dreamt tonight.

Brushing the town in fused colour,

Walking on heavy grief despite,

Breezes shift around my collar,

Opalescent path dreamt tonight.

Can a lost soul be one again,

When a drab town worship its height?

Drowning in dry neglected pain,

Opalescent path dreamt tonight.

Poetic Form: Kyrielle

A French poetic form. Followed by 8 syllables with a rhyme scheme of abab by refraining the last line.

Bundle Of Joy (A Tribute to My Son Like Nephew)

There was once a sarcastic boy,

He can never be your play toy.

Playing tricks on the old,

While treating them as gold,

Shy little bundle of fine joy.

Crack Sheep

Oh dahlin's of the universe,

Who fail to throw a fit of curse,

Like a baba crack sheep,

Who haha like a creep,

Amused as you try to converse.

Beautiful Sluterry

Once upon a damn fuckery,

Lived a beautiful sluterry;

Fragrance so mind blowing,

So proudly just showing,

Made my eyes so damn watery.

Poetic Form (For above three): Limerick. Limericks is a form of verse usually humorous and frequently rude.in five line,with a strict rhyme scheme as AABBA and syllable count as 8,8,6,6,8. Follow the metre.

Flames of Lust

When the morning stars

Lit his soul on flames of lust,

I blew his feelings with dust

Poetic Form: Katauta

A Japanese form of poetry with syllables 5,7,7 or 5,7,5 with no rhyme scheme.

Flourished Tonight

Warmth under the cold northern lights

In search of the stars in your eyes,

Drifting to a cold blooming bliss,

Catching a flame inside your soul.

Hush as the moon watched you slow dance,

Warmth under the cold northern lights.

Love flourished at its deepest sins,

Counting constellations of us.

Grasses embedding our cold skin,

Reflecting neon lights on our lips,

Warmth under the cold northern lights,

Happy echoes in time we made.

Truth found under the glowing sky,

Blazing elegance of our touch;

So gently aligned once again,

Warmth under the cold northern lights.

Poetic Form: Quatern

A French poetic form with four quatrains, 8 syllables and refrains.

A Fool's Validation

When you fat shamed the kid across the room,

When you lurked around for the fruity juices,

And fooling the views in a perfect groom.

When you left the abuse chained in bruises,

Was the pain not enough validation,

Rejecting your kin's empty refuses?

Skipping from every wild confrontation,

Playing never have I ever done so,

Raising minions full of expectation.

I pitied your nose in the backyard whoa,

So let go of the pretend act you show.

Poetic Form: Terza Rima

Italian verse form with stanzas of tercets followed by a two line stanza.

Aba, bcb, cdc .. 10 syllables.

The Fox

Nemesis,

My dahlin' full of sly diss,

Your barks echo like the fox,

Box.

A ghost mind,

Fooling the innocent blind,

If only you stayed in line,

Fine.

Poetic Form: Deibide Baise Fri Toin
Irish form of poetry (syllables 3,7,7,1) following a rhyme scheme of a,a,b,b.

Worst Halfwit

Question, do we always play our part,

Art,

Dancing through our mindless imagination,

On,

When our encrypted tricks are laughable,

Able,

Swept under the illusionary dill,

Ill,

Let no breeze take us to a star,

Far,

And I turned into the creep simply senseless,

Less,

Yet you mocked me as the worst halfwit,

It,

I smile to the stillness of a calm tease,

Ease.

Poetic Form: Echo verse

No syllables, just an echo of the last word of each line and repeat the end syllable of each line.

Hell, No Whine!

Are their "pure" intentions aligned,
Questions in mind,
You breathing fine,
Staying in line.

To you, it seems a naïve beach,
Who failed in speech,
Cover for cost,
Thinking we lost.

Shame in the truth you could not speak,
Vicious spell freak,
Drunk on your shine,
It's hell no whine.

Poetic Form: Minute Poem

3 quatrains, 8 syllables first line of each stanza, 4 syllables in the remaining lines of each stanza, rhyme scheme: aabb, ccdd, eeff. Follow the iambic meter.

Russet Prints

Russet leaves,

Petal prints,

Blissful blends.

Starry knights

Moves the sky

More to wish.

Let the moon

Be my eyes

Purple hues.

Poetic Form: Tricube
Three stanzas with three lines and three syllables.
No rhyme scheme.

The Fall

It's true that everybody falls sometimes,

Questions of seeing this coming fades.

Smile for the memories we've made at times,

Mind your survival as it upgrades.

Counting your blessings that slipped from your thought,

But let's not avoid the demons we've fought.

Praying for the beautiful night sky as calm,

As we take a step killing all the harm.

Poetic Form: Rispetto
An Italian poetic form with two stanzas, rhyme scheme of abab, ccdd, following a syllable count of 10.

Faded

Love, the key that sets you free,

Fading to a complex mind,

As the silent lullaby

Of I'm not your fool.

Poetic Form: Dodoitsu
Fixed folk song form of Japanese origin, often about love or humour. Syllables: 7,7,7,5.

Playful Touches

Play push and alone,

You missing and gone.

Sinful

Dreams of fresh loved moan,

Oh you should have known

Playful

Touches, oh, come on!

Yes, sweet air you've blown,

Graceful.

Poetic Form: Lai
French form. Consists of 9 lines.
Aabaabaab. 5 syllables for a, 2 syllables for b.

Creep To You

Forgive my blunt forthcoming, my love,

Letting our fatal dreams crawl in.

Memories of tomorrow,

A vicious time kill. Hey,

I'm drowning in these,

Painful blindness.

A love gone

So deep

In

To

Frozen

Lullabies,

Which kept me sane

When I drifted in

Your words of pure wisdom,

And your cheeky humor of

That broken summer which creeped you.

Don't be scared of the words that remain.

Poetic Form: Nonet (Double Nonet)
Follows the syllables 9,8,7,6,5,4,3,2,1. Known to be the nine line countdown poem.

Chain Of Thoughts

Did you really think I would loathe you in my own despair,

Or did you choose to suffocate in your own memories of pain?

Nah Dahlin', don't get it twisted with your tripping chain of thoughts.

Poetic Form: Sijo

A Korean verse form with three lines, each line consisting of at least 14-16 syllables, with the second line often the longest.

Truth of Sighs

Angelic devil,

Found in a pool of madness,

We painted our fate on stars.

Will it ever dawn

To a steam of clarity,

Shaded behind the shy moon?

Have we lost our shine,

Running in circles of cries,

Hanging on our truth of sighs?

Poetic Form: Choka

3 tercets

Syllables : 5,7,7 5,7,7 5,7,7

Do You Hear Me

We spoke love to the stars when they glistened through the stillness of silence.

Poetic form: Monoku

17 syllables, one line.

Owls Of Sham

Your soil is a haven of venomous berries, that's sham;

Misleading the seeds of doubts as thirst of worries, that's sham.

Articulating fables of fetishes that varies,

Conspiring a smooth voyage with evil fairies,
that's sham.

Promising salvation found in the lore of my diaries,

Surrounded by the outlawed lying canaries,
that's sham.

Torturous afflictions to forbidden tender cherries,

Owls woken up in haste through blazed midday queries, that's sham.

Within the caves of your truth rests those dark theories,

Deceiving seasons cloaking near discoveries,
that's sham.

Poetic Form: Ghazal

An Arabic form of poetry, the origin also falls into Indian subcontinent, which express the pain of losing or waiting for someone you love. It has two refraining words with a rhyme scheme of AA, BA, CA, DA, EA.

A syllable count of 14.

It consists of no lesser than 5 couplets.

Crime In Sin

But after all this wait in time dahlin'

We are still called a crime in sin.

Poetic form: Couplet
Two lines that rhyme and have identical metres.

Sweet Farewell

A

Gain

Again

The silence,

The violent screams

Reek within the air around you

The final counting of the sweet farewell, my dahlin'.

Can't you see I have been haunted by your heartless whispers breezing so confusingly?

Poetic Form: Fibonacci

Follows a syllable count of 1, 1, 2, 3, 5, 8, 13, 21.

Unconditional Love (A Tribute to My Beautiful Sister)

Best

Times in

Life are the

Moments we laughed,

Undefeated by

Shades which never

Faded in

To the

Worst.

Poetic Form: Ninette
Nine line poem. The first and second line could be same or synonyms or antonyms. Following the Syllables 123454321.

Maybe Sometimes

If only you knew

I died a little inside,

Sometimes or maybe.

Poetic Form: Senryu
Similar to haiku. The syllable count is 5,7,5 following three lines. It is also a Japanese form of poetry. However, the difference between haiku and senryu is that senryu is humorous and states a fact whereas haiku is mostly of nature and more serious.

Courageous Loving (Tribute to my beautiful sister!)

Porcelain heart is beautiful,

Kind gestures so wonderful.

Jukebox songs of her courageous,

Burning souls of the outrageous.

Her warm embrace so promising,

Close to home, waiting and wishing.

Embroidered her ribs to loving,

While she exhaled smiles by caring.

Poetic Form: Cyhyded fer
Couplets with eight syllables.

Constellations Of Memories

Sturdy vermillion that takes my breath to the stars,

Sky sparked filled with constellations of memories,

Electrifying blinks tethering in my haste dreams,

Built walls within walls of unburnt solitary,

When moon lit your dreamy eyes with untold stories.

Them Slender Vortex closing in my spiral scars,

Ceramic streaks of your touch from the galaxies;

Embracing me in love to flow as scarlet streams,

Golden tints engraved to your soul as wild berry;

Remember it as withered windblown time series.

Mischievous sun and moon continue to vary,

With masked hoes drawn as untouchable sly fairies.

Poetic form : Rimas Dissolutas

French form of poetry. Uses 12 syllables in five line stanzas followed by an envoy.

Rhyme scheme :

1-A

2-B

3-C

4-D

5-E

6-A

7-B

8-C

9-D

10-E

Envoy

D

E)))

Blind Trickery

A poison feasting on my innocence,
Words mismatch as I mould in poetry;
When forever never made any sense,
The petty plots of their blind trickery.

Hell bent to flatter them leaving a scar,
Destroyed by the weight of their monster eyes,
That darkness haunted, draining me so far,
Dreams of unforgiven pain in disguise.

How you wrecked me from ruins to rebirth,

As you mocked my rooted tears shed in fear,

Leaving all crumbs of deceit on this earth,

Pretty lies and fake smiles is all I hear.

Fatal dreams as I read between those lies,

So boost your ego, counting on my cries!

Form of Poetry: Sonnet
It is a form of poetry with 10 syllables per line, consisting of 14 lines with a rhyme scheme of abab, cdcd, efef and followed by a couplet gg.
You could also follow the aa bb rhyme scheme.

Cold Machine Heart

Chose to sneak through, hoping that it would phase,

Hiding behind razor thin glass, you fool,

The Cold machine heart of a double face,

Define insanity as if it's cool,

Cumulating these tears and smiles in trace,

When sour betrayals were your biggest tool,

Life according to an immoral brain,

You found humor from injecting dark pain.

Poetic form : ottava rima

(8 lines with 10 syllables, rhyme scheme: abababcc)

Inevitable Distance

Bitter cold distance between us,

We go back to how they discuss

Our love in slow motion,

As the inevitable truth,

At the peak of our thirst for youth,

Swept beneath the ocean.

Poetic form: rime couee
(French six line stanzas, rhyme scheme: AABCCB,
syllable count: 886886)

Your Golden Rays

My mind goes back to rainy days;

I would bury myself in you,

With our lips sealed to the best view,

Glowing under the golden rays.

Blowing my heart in mystic ways

Embraced me as your only skin,

No space to lay in deadly sin,

Time traveled frozen through oceans,

Carrying waves of emotions,

Let these sheer lights reach for the win.

Poetic form: Espinela
(A Spanish poetic form with one four line stanza and one 6 line stanza, each line consisting of 8 syllables, rhyme scheme: abba/accddc)

Forgotten Crime

All those words were meaningless,

When you thought I'd be grieving?

Holding on pointless drama,

Those scriptures were found to be deceiving.

Shame on you for hopes of trust,

Depriving you of my time,

Dusted flashbacks that remained,

And you truly became a forgotten crime.

Poetic Form: Endecha
Spanish quatrain form with the rhyme scheme abcb. Syllable count of 7 in line 1, 2 and 3, followed by 11 syllables in the 4th line.

Blood Bath

Counting every death,
Symphony of my breath,
Left losing all our strength,
When they could rob our wealth

Dreaming as on meth,
You sober minds in depth,
Washed in a cold blood bath,
Silent hunger in stealth

Poetic Form: Breccbairdne poem
Irish quatrain with four line stanzas, five syllable in the first line, six syllables in the other three lines, each line ending with two syllable words, where lines two and four rhyme. All end words consonate.

Delusional Cellar

If only you knew the me before you

Twists of the good the bad and the ugly,

Oh the sound of music,

Rushing in so continuously,

Delusional clueless story teller,

Ink dried in a mysterious cellar,

Written differently,

I had the urge to be reborn as someone new.

Poetic Form: Mistress Bradstreet stanzas

Syllable count: 10,10,6,8,10,10,6,12

Rhyme Scheme: abcbddba

An 8-line stanza

Father

For

All the

Times

He reminded me to say no to

Evil and to

Remain far from the cruel world.

Poetic Form: Acrostic

The Mermaid’s Kiss

She woke up in the middle of the night from the most magnificent dream of her life. She was a mermaid. Her pale skin was luminous and a cloud of long black hair trailed behind her like streaks of ink swirling in water. She could sense exotic marine creatures following the trail of her pursuit. She sighed and wondered how late it was, and whether this was a good dream. It turned into a nightmare in a blink that changed her life.

Here in the arms of the sea,
I swam ten feet under to a garden I see,
Capturing the beauty of a world so free,
The cold and the warmth of colours I agree,

Humongous sharks moving as a show,
I was a mermaid kissing the turtles so slow,
When the red and blue fishes danced, wow,
In my mind, I stored them low,

I moan an echoing scream,
Indeed I cannot escape this,
This pestilent torment of dreams,
You are ringing in my ears,
As you wake me in my sleep,
Now it's gone too deep

From a beautiful dream to a nightmare so sore,
Where sad eyed mermaid tossed in slumbers,
Nightmare dreams, no mortal mind could hold as she tumbles,
Sadness in the heart,
Like a storm that ripped apart,
Moon is shining down,
Into the deep it's so cold,
And I wear a frown,
Lonely the mermaid untold.

Poetic Form: Free Verse

Dear Haters!

There is no reason for debate,

When they say haters are gonna hate,

Quick to question my pen's sincerity,

So tell me about your throne of integrity,

You claim to be one who follows god's way,

But this is where hypocrisy comes into play,

Are wrath, envy and pride not seen as a sin?

But your two faced judgement seems to make you grin,

The truth is I don't give a shit my dahlin',

But today I'm giving two cents without a warning,

Choose your words wisely, that's what they say,

Do I care? When my life is my own runway,

Watch my spirit fly higher, baby,

I can tell it's driving you crazy,

Your quarrels and shallow thinking cannot define me,

Venomous words will only refine what I choose to be,

Bathe in it joker, as I have the last laugh,

Because you only read my story in half,

There is a stinking stench toxicating your tongue,

Like a herd of cows left to die in a field of dung.

Poetic Form: Free Verse

Stalking Star

The stalking star,

Gazes from afar,

Shooting so bizarre,

Dripping like black tar,

Admiring every sigh,

Crafty like a fox so sly,

Alert to each grasp and cry,

Like an infatuated spy,

Predator hunting in the night,

Making her the sun that beams so bright,

Confused between wrong and right,

Obsession had led to spite,

An online spider web spinner,

This feast is not yet your dinner,

Deception makes you a sinner,

For this heart you are no winner!

Poetic form: free verse

Yesterday's Pain

A radiant vermilion swept across the summer sky,

The fragrance of romance danced through velvety streaks of her hair,

Swerving swiftly within rhythmic notes of her sunset lullabies,

She was stunned as she stumbled upon a tremor so wild,

Laughed and brushed it off while yesterday's pain still lingered on,

One might say she have reached her madness,

Refusing to believe that the walls were closing in,

Frozen by peculiar invasions across her sweet scarlet skies,

She tries to merge with the scorching colours that seemed so mild,

Wishing they would give a blind eye to every rush of pain,

Breathing the infected air of her nemesis,

Hoping she could shake the impossible as her habits were accustomed to,

Knowing that she shall not stay down defeated with as she did fall,

And the wrath of her clap back would be a new dawn of hope.

Poetic Form: Free Verse

Overcoming Anxiety and Depression!

With every sunrise glimmering on your skin,

Let it soak in with a reason to try again,

It would feel like there is no reason to walk that walk,

When all you do is talk that talk,

Fine!

It is reasonable to sink right onto the fall,

To lift your ass out of bed is another crawl,

Anxiety and depression,

A demonic Satan which tries to overpower your aggression,

Are you willing to fight the slump,

Or would you just swim away with the bump?

It is okay to cry that cry, laugh that laugh, frown that frown.

The winner will fight the devil,

Courage to overcome with a murky back,

A weighty intellect, finding it hard to utter a word,

Breaking down with the memory of every dawn.

But!

Let there be rays of inspiration,

Using your faith, morals, ethics, beliefs as your weapon,

Building mighty comebacks I would reckon!

Poetic Form: Free verse

To be Continued...

It always start nearly the same,

A whisk of an intense blow of change, without a warning lines begin to fade,

Stuck in a loop of time just for a second longer,

Reliving a rewinded moment helplessly looking for the ripples to blame,

This is when my hand reaches out for a sense of comfort,

A hope of serenity,

This is the moment as my mind unfolds into a quill of poetry,

Pious vultures of the mad devil never stopped intruding,

For a moment I let myself heap into the scattered gems of illusions,

And let my heart rest from the worldly obligations.

I believe the world is a cage full of lunacy,

So I gave my mind a sense of clarity,

Forgiving myself for taking a dip into the lost sea,

Quietly pleading for my own mercy,

While finally seizing the reality along the tides,

Standing at the crest of my prime,

Listening to the whispers of the calm rain drops.

There was a time when fake looked real and real looked fake,

A cruel play called the fraud of reality,

Then the silence refined every curve, every edge through blinding shadows,

Letters from the ghosts full of deceptive "how are you's,"

Making a mockery out of my lessons naming it karma,

When the truth is,

These familiar streets are filled with stained pavements, covered in dark history, I know all too well,

In time I found my patience focused on a birth of light as an inevitable strength,

Be the fall of rays through the darkling wickedness,

It may seem as if it is a closing of a show,

But to find that the parade must go on,

And a warrior of unexpected storms.

My armour is bound with thorns I spent decades plucking out of my chest;

Now watch me unleash the beast inside,

As you read my "tip of the iceberg" confessions.

Heed this; you have not seen the last of me...

Poetic Form: Free Verse

Once again…

Listen to me,

The quiet rebellion of the gentle storm,

Staying lost in scriptures of our full moon release,

Don't be surprised,

In these pages you will find an addictive obsession,

A muse which brought me back to home again,

As you whispered about beauty in the broken,

She whispered three words,

Suffocating the senses,

While burning the bay leaves,

Letting him take over her broken soul,

Washing away the tears and filling her guts with desire,

She was lost in a sight of love again.

Poetic form: free verse

You can always go back

You can always go back,

To remember what you have survived,

To build a fortress in your mind,

Gather all the horses you have felt along the way,

For you are not just a survivor, my dahlin',

But a warrior

Hunting for a prey to feed on.

Poetic Form: Free Verse

Bohemian Aroma

As hail of stones stripped away her unshed tears,

She found faith through aesthetic lines of her marble walls,

To tick away the voodoo dirt that still broils her breathing toes,

Nostalgic fumes of bohemian aroma filled up hollow lungs,

And the devil's ivy swerved to the misleading euphony,

Conjuring a summoning hell through what they thought was paradise,

Gasping for answers in the crevices of a smothering foul charm,

A purveyor of an occultist, who found themselves to be quite the tool,

Pretending to have unlocked a nefarious power so untouchable,

One would wish it was irreversible,

For all those grace seemed effortlessly reassuring,

As if they meant no harm while they revived an organic portion jinxed with poison,

Planting evil coincidences, in hopes of blending into pearly clouds,

Though they were one among the empty hearted succubus,

Latching themselves onto the satanic moth disguised as a butterfly,

Cloaked in linen and silk with shards of sins dripping from their lips,

Yet when the sun and moon merged together,

They refused to grasp the reality that gushed through her purple veins,

The truth that held knives and was not an open path for every imbecile creature.

Poetic Form: Free Verse

Curiosity

Overwhelmed with strangeness,

When everything is endless,

Overviewing a star left aimless,

When surrounded by snakes who are faithless,

Overpowered by a pool of ego yet so graceless,

When every move became so shameless,

Overshadowed by the demons that were nameless,

When the memories turned out to be pointless,

Overcrowded by the actions of heartless,

When kindness is simply just priceless,

Overdrained by the eyes which were worthless,
when nightmares were to be frameless,

Eyes lurking around, through curiosity and steadiness.

Poetic Form: free verse

Stars In Time

You were a fountain of love,

Touched me so deep,

Wishing the show would never end,

Came back to the time our eyes met,

As you held me in your arms,

Like you would never let go,

Love me a little longer,

A tad bit more than we ever planned to,

Or let us fall back to the dreams,

Aligned with the stars in time.

Poetic Form: Free Verse

Let's Heal

Let the stars and the sky,

Witness our moment of healing,

A second of you and I,

I cannot withdraw from.

My Pen, My Ink

My pen didn't bleed,

My pain healed,

It sewed me up from within,

With every stroke of the pen,

My wounds started closing,

Which were once open,

The words which came out of my firing rage became the water which subsided the fierce fiery flames.

My ink held secrets,

Secrets of the moments we left behind,

Some of them hurt,

While some made us fly,

The truth is,

Words are words,

Only a writer would understand the depth of it,

The rest proved their hypocrisy through action,

Action which failed to go hand with scripts,

Let my pen and my ink flow,

Until I feel like myself again.

Poetic form: free verse

Life-lihood

All our traumas made us monsters,

Monsters wearing human skin.

We gave up on "seem to be tough" fights,

Fights we could've fought to win.

From losing sleep to losing the precious ones,
The precious ones to whom we are praying.

Praying for just a minute of peace,
Peace which we wish would stay.

And the joy demised under false circumstances,
Circumstances that we face always.

Indeed, I agree that life is full of complications,
Complications that we bleed through our pen.

Poetic form : free verse/loop poem

Flashbacks

Verse 1:

For turning you invisible,

I'll always be regretful,

When things got critical

Was easy to be forgetful.

I left you in a state of shock,

In tears heavier than a rock.

I heard you, but left you on mute,

Now you know I'm forbidden fruit.

Chorus:

Just another day without me,

Can't you see I set you free.

I know I killed your dreams,

But now you flow like streams.

Verse 2:

The bed we laid in got colder,

Things changed as we grew older.

Waves of thoughts lost their way,

As silence ruined every day,

But, I still hate how you hold her,

Because sometimes I miss how we were.

Pre chorus:

These feelings I just let them slide,

Although I fight against those tides,

I loved how we used to glide,

Oh! At times it was a good ride,

Just another day without me,

Can't you see I set you free.

I know I killed your dreams,

But now you flow like streams.

Verse 3:

Flashbacks can be an intrusion,

So I throw stones at your illusion.

I gave our love a conclusion,

As life was full of confusion,

My mind was fighting delusion,

So I gave my soul seclusion.

Chorus:

Just another day without me,

Can't you see I set you free.

I know I killed your dreams,

But now you flow like stream.

Poetic Form: Lyrical Form

Unchanged

Times have changed,

Because minds have changed,

But one thing stays unchanged,

Being unknown by the people

We thought we have known.

Poetic Form: Free Verse

Quotes By Me

I would rather silently leave than violently stay.

When you already know that forever is only a memory which we engraved in our flashbacks on repeat.

People will always remember that one wrong despite all the many rights. That's when they fail.

The only thing left for you to receive is to forgive yourself before you forgive them.

You said you were heartless; so now, I treat you like you are.

Pitched you with the highest star while I bitched about you to the moon! That too is a type.

Many doors closed on me before I closed the door
on many.

Acknowledgement

First, I would like to take a moment to thank God for blessing me with patience, strength, courage and hope. Every day the power of my faith grows stronger as I witness your miracles through my darkest and brightest times. Without the prayers and constant reminder of God, I would not have been able to come this far.

To the sun, the moon, the stars, the mountains, the ocean and the greens for inspiring me to continuously dream and to stay focused.

My deepest appreciation goes to my beautiful sister. Thank you for being at my side every day. I have always been a writer, and it has always been my dream to one day publish my own book. I would not have been able to do it without my sister introducing me to the writing community and inspiring me to learn new poetic forms and polish my writing skills. So, thank you for everything, thank you for your love and support always. Thank you for being you and I love you! I can't imagine a day without you.

To my handsome, smart and intelligent son like nephew. Your sense of humour and sarcasm keeps me going every day. I love you from the bottom of my heart. Thank you for being patient at my worst and for always giving me the best advice!

To my mother, for always introducing me to interesting books that inspire me. Thank you for guiding me and being a good friend a listener and mentor. Thank you for everything and I love you.

To my father, for supporting me during my worst times in life. For giving me hope and inspiring me to always "see no evil, say no evil and hear no evil." Thank you for everything.

To my beautiful, most supportive cousin who has helped me to design my book cover. Thank you for always being my security at my weakest times, for making me laugh and keeping me positive even through the darkest of times. For carrying me like your backpack when I couldn't walk. For staying up through the nights, laughing along with me through the pain, for always staying connected and being loyal and true to me. Thank you. And I love you!

To everyone who has prayed for me, checked up on me or dropped a text of encouragement during my tough times and good times.

To the silence. You brought out the emotions in me musically.

To my photographer for constantly being a support. Thank you for being there through the highs and down lows in life. Every minute is cherished!

To the American pie who has been there for me during my worst time. Thank you for years of friendship. You have taught me much!

To my uncles, aunts, cousins, family and friends. Thank you! And I love you!

To my cousin, Am. Thank you for inspiring me with your strength and courage. I love you and your amazing kids always.

To all the doctors who patiently guided me through my struggles. For making me feel comfortable and cared for. For answering my texts any time of the day during the treatment. Thank you!

To the Doctor who dives, thank you!

To my healer, who is a survivor, for teaching me to think positively and to never look back on the days I have lost. Instead, to look forward to the days I will be at ease. Thank you! You are and will be remembered for your support and care. The fallen angel.

To all the new amazing talented writer friends I have met through the writing community. Thank you for sharing your knowledge. Sometimes we meet people through words and they make a great impact.

Thank you, Nilay. You are an amazing writer and a great friend. Thank you for always making me laugh and being there for me through the healing journey.

A special thanks to the silent one, Poetic gardener, for supporting me and guiding me by sharing years of knowledge and wisdom. Thank you for your prayers and for treating me like a little sister and for collaborating.

You will always be appreciated for being there throughout my healing.

To my friend from India, Zaina Ahmed, for the spontaneous amazing work together on the mermaid's kiss, the one I would treasure always.

To my friend word.sly for always making me laugh and collaborating on lifelihood.

To my friend Ms. Adyasha Rout for collaborating on my pen my ink. We always flow so well together.

To every heartbreak, every betrayal, every nightmare, every failure, every victory which articulated into forms of poetry. Thank you!

To you, reader, for taking out time to read my book and acknowledging it. I appreciate it and I hope this book has helped you to dream a little bit more.

To everyone who made this possible!

Appreciated!

Thank you!

9 789358 360080

Printed by Libri Plureos GmbH in Hamburg, Germany